EMPATHY PRESCRIBED

ELLA VEGA

ARCHWAY
PUBLISHING

Archway Publishing books may be ordered through booksellers or by contacting:

Archway Publishing
1663 Liberty Drive
Bloomington, IN 47403
www.archwaypublishing.com
844-669-3957

Interior Image Credit: Sergio Garzón

For more information on the author, please visit www.ellavegaauthor.com

ISBN: 978-1-6657-0057-3 (sc)
ISBN: 978-1-6657-0058-0 (hc)
ISBN: 978-1-6657-0056-6 (e)

Library of Congress Control Number: 2020925020

Print information available on the last page.

Archway Publishing rev. date: 02/16/2021

CONTENTS

The quantification of the World...1

The Peril of Life 5

Sober Faith 9

Empathy Prescribed 13

The Sweat on the Brow...17

Love Not Deserved..19

A Sun Dance Ago 21

The Blues...25

Prejudice..27

The Blame..29

Significance 33

Kaleidoscopic Joy 35

Elegy 37

Jazz Under the Rain 43

Grit 45

Summer's off...47

Juniper Sea 51

Once In a Blue Moon..53

The Synthesis of You and Me...57

The Zombie of Me...59

Blue 61

Desert's Displeasure 63

Steadfast wind...67

Old libel...69

Thief at Night 71

About the Poems in This Book 73

Acknowledgments 99

To my children, Priscilla and Samuel,
you inspire me to create and achieve.
To my high-school Spanish teacher, Don Victor,
your persistence and passion for perfection
are the reason I fell in love with words.

THE QUANTIFICATION OF THE WORLD

It all started with time
the day turned into night
a continuation of life's flow
based on the quantity of light
contriving how much is owed.

Thus, currency is involved
granted, the need for a measure
to barter adhering to fairness
obvious consequence to some: treasure
and to others desolate scantness.

It all started with a need
and who extinguishes paucity
aiding destitute who share grunts
fallen, unfortunate in scarcity
all those prey to life's cruel hunts.

Consequence of one extreme
is the greed in creating more wealth
nothing is nearly enough for myself
not sparing even a few
for the unfortunate matter of you.

By contrast, there is martyrdom
a competition of benefactors
God forbid someone's own need
requires for you not to bleed
justness not even a factor.

Clear as water, one can see
everything is quantifiable:
the abstract, the concrete, the what if
but the measure of reality
no matter how stiff
is at the end, highly unreliable.

THE PERIL OF LIFE

The Peril of life
the half-truth, unforgiving:
are we living, or dying?
Is there honest purpose underlying?

Is the clock's fixating sound
the sole reason of our here and how?
Or is there a profound degree
of things unseen and divine decree?

On one hand, life's sport is raw
a dice's fling, a chance's law
on the other, tight as rope
where there lies judgement
but also hope.

One circus is sure
to be tightrope without net
displaying ironic acrobatics
audience be fools, filled with dramatics
performer's heart full of regret.

The other show of bizarre puppeteering
where you act hanging from a thread
surrounded by eyes with no head
puppet's soul safe and God-fearing.

So, what is it going to be, you ask me?
Fearful kinetics with no intention?
Or a dire waiting for intervention?

The best seat to take
in this reckless spectacle
is the seat in the middle front row
balance hopeful, but skeptical
soaring high, but preying low.

SOBER FAITH

Sober faith, I'm telling you!
Not distortion of the mind
by creating false expectations
as to leave it all behind.

Sober, unadulterated faith
understanding of one's chance
by placing emphasis on purpose
and on taking a last stance.

Faith abiding in strove focus
in plague's panic, certainty prevails
putting an end to pharaoh's locusts
hazy to some, to others unfailing.

Faith mature, champions command
like a battle wound in the mend
not eased on a banal demand
taking its time to alleviate.

Next step too soon, I'm telling you,
faith should guide whatever most
not because of desperation
but regardless of the cost.

Be reckless when falling,
relentlessness as guide
for failure is first
perceived in the mind.

EMPATHY PRESCRIBED

Empathy prescribed
to progress and disagree
without iniquities or conflict
to exist together while being me.

For what is war
if not a consequence
of long settled division?
The result of fearful thinking
that radicals label as treason?

And what is ignorance
but the incompetence
of those who pretend to know?
who can't reach out without prejudice
and instead punch a hard blow?

Tolerant behavior
as opposed to shallow word
that is vomited with ridicule
piercing squire with the sword.

In one picture there is sacrifice
without expecting a return
in the other, nothing will suffice
they will gladly see you burn.

So, choose carefully your discourse
let alone your execution
for you don't know everything
and the world is prompt to confusion.

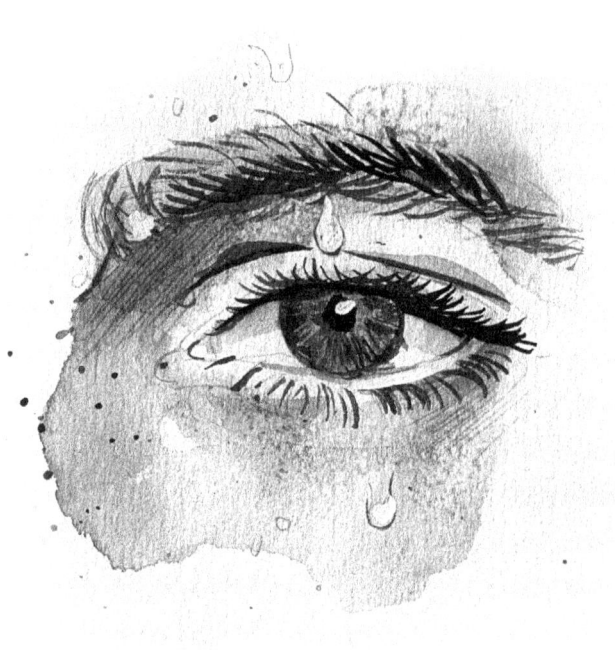

THE SWEAT ON THE BROW

Pounding...
moving...
coming along.
Regardless of needs
or discernment from wrong.
No easy way to foretell where it leads.
No need to say if it's tiresome or long.
Such is the sweat
that pours down the brow
there to pay the debt
like a ring and a vow.

LOVE NOT DESERVED

As long as you go
and create something new
I grant no affliction
of not having a clue.

I dread seeing in your eyes
a stiffness of breath
a lack of vitality
an emotional death.

So, go on, intend to wander
set sail even under thunder
pursue that blasphemous measure
of lack of love and wasteful treasure.

For if you linger, I tremble
at the thought of your decay
vanity has issued temple
in your heart, each time you stay.

As for me, I got emptiness
not knowing to forfeit
with, I'm sure, less heaviness
than granting your soul a hard hit.

A SUN DANCE AGO

A sun dance ago
unmeasurable wealth
maybe pain as abysmal as darkness
maybe joy explosive within oneself.

But how can this birth
of a nameless offspring
be fruitful through one's sorrow
turning it into a better tomorrow?

A sure dose of divine inspiration
a cup full of knowledge in mind
maybe just raising to the occasion
a horse's blinker to make it blind.

Regardless of recipe
undeniable as it is
art is born into creation...
divine child's butterfly kiss.

Living with fear of dying
is itself the worst possible death.
You, not even trying
direly saving for your last breath.

THE BLUES

The harmonica is crying
a tune with much soul
it's warmth intervening
when life's weather is cold.

Melancholy floods
the sound of history untold;
guitars aching and bouncing
looking for someone to hold.

And as the voice whispers
a loud sound undisclosed
the ear hardly hears
what the mind finds predisposed.

And so, the music plays
nostalgia's dire love tune
wakes the best and worst in people
like a werewolf during full moon.

PREJUDICE

Life recorded on a tape
a premature cut of hate
for our perspective has much flaws
while we think of it as law.

The past fired up a blazing iron
branded poorly a grotesque icon
now the future sight is bleak
for fear is close and soul is weak.

Prejudice creeps right in
survival instinct at its worst
optimistic surely to win
subjectivity's clear burst.

But uniqueness cruel game
is sometimes its greatest glory
for if everyone were same
there'll be no intriguing story.

THE BLAME

"Generally speaking"
says Snobby
while speaking over mic
to avoid those pointing fingers
and to feel he is always right.

"I'm a victim!"
cries Neglectful
to avoid being at fault
when society is to blame
his progress can excusably halt.

"It's my life!"
Selfish argues
common opinion on his script
to ensure no responsibility
follows his deceit.

At all times subsequent
displays of boiling psyche
an inclination towards ego
nothing matters but to lie.

And all the rest just have to follow
and expect to gratify
those demagogues and radicals
who wish to magnify.

An average inquiry in a human being in the past, a lifetime's pursuit. Today, a few seconds of probing, suddenly, I'm an expert at it too?

SIGNIFICANCE

Abstract and innumerable
like cosmic dust weighted in space
like figure's shadow, midnight dark
banishing without a trace.

Void of pain or misuse
like energy in ancient star
or a planet worth researching
notwithstanding how far.

How do we find such rarity
while being able to take such toll?
Setting ourselves up for failure
and withstanding our own fall?

Significance...

Heavy metal from foreign orb
familiar to privileged, foreign to some
sweet, successful, full of purpose
like an astronaut arriving home.

KALEIDOSCOPIC JOY

Of bright hues, fantastic figures
novelty delight as one just quivers
expecting whimsical creations
waking curious sensations.

Like a child at carnival
who has found their favorite pal
everything bright, everything fair
just the two playing in a pair.

Capricious to appear
utopia's perfect bliss
untouched, all you hold dear
nothing wanted or amiss.

One rejoices and then questions
how to remain in pleasing joy?
How to avoid darkness suggestions?
How did the maker build the toy?

Kaleidoscope's optical illusion
just glass and playful mood
serving joy's lesson and conclusion
that it's mostly us choosing we should.

ELEGY

Supper hanging on the table
not a single soul to blame
digestion painful and disabled
reality just sank in today.

Is not the vanity of a quarrel
nor the stress of obligation
tonight's morsel has proven queasy
it's ingestion troublesome, uneasy.

We brace ourselves against the throb
dreading the time when we must sob
instability according to plan:
life expired in a man.

Fear caves in, certain as grief
the past the present, the what if
all while we wait in that dark place
wishing, but knowing it isn't the case.

Next day, granted, we hardly rest
comes with decisions and emotions
dressed in black, we wait the test
of a ritual full of commotion.

We say goodbye to that one man
that held the whole world on his shoulders
and we progress to become
the brand-new orphans and loners.

There's one permanent golden truth
of undeniable positivity:
the great chance to have called dad
the best man this lost world had.

Life is looking in the mirror
setting who you want to be
then fighting your present self
in order to actually become free.

JAZZ UNDER THE RAIN

Cadence pace with rhythm
breathing jazz under the rain
with her unsuspected greatness
at University Lane.

Black umbrella in her hand
gray drizzle, narrow path
time now in high demand
between biology and math.

Figure petite, soaking shoes
tuning to that wistful sound
in a scene well-suited
for a modest college town.

Aiming high, that inner flame
against all her limitations
singing in the rain
nostalgic scene with implications.

While overhearing trumpets
not a single step in vain
surrounded by brick buildings
there, at University Lane.

GRIT

First-responder soldier
in a hard to battle war
knows odds aren't in his favor
but keeps taking it too far.

Pride is hurt, eyes are red
tears from brothers full of lead
he manages to catch momentum
for the fighting down ahead.

Demoralizing calamity
present company excluded
sets a change of mentality
for failure is better disputed.

And so, it is, the mental picture
of first-responder grit:
knows his own limitations
but never how to quit.

SUMMER'S OFF

Summer's off
a colder breeze beneath main spotlight
sunset pounding at the door
a child's ethos changes focus
although left starving for more.

Autumn of a childhood
time to leave capers behind
and face the harsh reality
of controlling one's own mind.

Colors changing on the landscape
no more idle recreation
now the leaves are falling
and responsibility is calling.

As the days end sooner
adulthood takes center stage
ending the boy's juvenile mindset
at his coming of age.

Patience is unequivocally
success' greatest asset
for the ability to wait for glory
is grit's all-time best story.

JUNIPER SEA

Glass half broken, don't you see
Juniper's mind living by the sea
often delighted in life's pleasure flair
parading with her precious nose in the air
acquaintance-filled extravagant domain
children were mainly her burdened complain.

Sumptuous procession, Juniper's class
forever hiring music from brass
and now sits alone, gulping tea
alone is Juniper, by the sea.

Charade of thorns, life's lecture pain
when disease visited her figure
it struck her gold and face disfigured
her beauty gone, no one remained.

Forlorn of comfort
stripped of pride
with absolutely nothing left to hide
and that's how loneliness became her
her mind in the past, Juniper Sea.

ONCE IN A BLUE MOON

At the junction of moment and sight
a lightbulb of genius engraves the unique
brainstorming concepts under candlelight
lie schemes for ideas to take flight.

Symposium of choices, together with skill
shut eyes to fear of rejection or pain
for good fortune alone doesn't satisfy thrill
embracing this basis leaves nothing to gain.

Like railway machine, full speed ahead
but instead of chassis lies your bare head
a railroad switch, no rod to hinder
suddenly stopping seems to be simpler.

But what to do about your precious freight?
Let it wither? Think of it tomorrow?
Forget completely that our time is borrowed?
Crush our dreams like we do with the crate?

Opportunity shows once in a blue moon
neglect predictions and avoid the guilt
ignore the psychic reading fortune
and show the material from which you're built.

The pain of ambivalence!
its frustration often too real!
broken record never stopped
unrepairable ordeal.

THE SYNTHESIS OF YOU AND ME

A full stomach after feast
on a most delightful banquet
congenial company to say the least
excellent view, no need for blanket
no hasting watch to tell time on wrist
that's how you and I coexist.

A well-planned expedition, cynosure of all eyes
no endeavor to perform, open itinerary
sojourning ancient ruins
pointless bringing gowns or ties
infinite funds to squander well passed the ordinary
no setbacks or mishaps and always energized
that's you and me, my love, the rest is secondary.

Chemicals that bind to create adhering matter
vital to humanity and impossible to scatter
unanimously living, blissful as can be
scheming sorrow out of life
the synthesis of you and me.

THE ZOMBIE OF ME

Creeping up like terminal disease
taking over the conscience of many
parasite's head begetting masterpiece
whose reality has shackles that are heavy.

What a misery it is to place ear
on vanity's enchanting whispers!
It rebukes everything you hold dear
enslaves you pass hands full of blisters.

Delusion erected by unsteady creature
comparing your treasure to mine
makes an idol of irrelevant feature
smashes everything thinking its fine.

The stench it creates!
Perceived from a distance
leaves victim presuming it smells like perfume
when in reality everyone's futile resistance
is to avoid the obvious toxic fumes.

As axiomatic as it appears to be
as derogatory its intentions portray
still it can create a zombie of me
and make me an enemy as soon as today.

BLUE

Is it blue
the color, deep beneath the sea?
Is its everchanging glory
a spectacular plea?
For it moves, and it rages
with unforgiving strength
It wants to tell us something:
states nothing is for free.

Have you heard the clamor
of fresh water's domain?
For it isn't blue, I heed,
sickness is its main complaint.

And if the waters roar,
for just reason they must rumble,
we are stewards who aren't humble...
hence material down the shores.

DESERT'S DISPLEASURE

Many deserts surrounding the soul
trials allure, regardless of ruse
sometimes hopeless, everyone confused
the ironic trick behind it all
for if peeking white flag to declare truce
life becomes pointless, no matter the call.

Coastal desert, Atacama:
far-off ocean's invitation
point of compass never lost
but that's when it hurts the most
for the unreachable destination
is in sight, but above one's station
seeking chance, no matter the cost.

Arid desert, The Sahara:
sand and heat are prelude
desolation consumes its guest
for if it wasn't for the quest
and the failure to conclude
life's humor wouldn't be so crude
brain's malfunction at its best.

Cold desert, The Antarctica:
surrounding iciness perceived
irrelevance makes one invisible
forcedly alone, with no one to give,
to help, to love, no matter the need
frost bite's victim, numb and miserable.

Why go through the displeasure
Of frustration, loneliness, depression?
Simply because, in between rough patches
There's an oasis worth the procession
And the deplorable never matches
Life's new perspective, a priceless possession.

STEADFAST WIND

Steadfast wind, the worst of traps
feels elusive to sail's arduous change
stagnation being its terrible result
a better version of me in exchange.

Stable draft, predictable weather
makes a sailor lazy to cruise
since he knows a storm isn't coming
oblivious because he has nothing to lose.

But what happens when the skies turn gray?
The sailor surely has to take position
he can no longer sit quietly and stay
or his fate will be wreck in collision.

Exact thoughts in life's cruel irony
for too cozy with comfort's condition
makes a drug out of safety and harmony
creates a premature end of voyage's mission.

Easy words to express and explain
but actually, being in the sailor's role
with the power to cease the rain
anyone would choose to avoid the toll
thus, sailing the journey in vain.

OLD LIBEL

The words are swept by the wind
irrepressibly and ruthlessly
it takes them away
no questions, nor shame.

Sterile words the ones you speak
no deepness, no love
unbearable and weak
leftovers from forgotten meal
gross to the taste
not enough to fill.

Selfish noise with deviant form
questions in motives that are clear as water
violating every etiquette norm
becoming an unfixable matter.

Old libel born from evil remark
leaving the two of us in the dark.

THIEF AT NIGHT

Restless thief in darkest night
ready, even though the breathing's heavy
silence guarding his own right
keen to take another's leavy.

Envy's climax holding on
justifying wrongful stance
never mind victim's own deeds
greed's dark spell turns into trance.

Like carnivore devouring prey
gutting, no reason to convey
martyr laying down in bed
wishing thief think of him dead.

When the ordeal is sealed and done
and treasure's pirate surely gone
what to do but pick the pieces
and ease a heart that has being torn?

ABOUT THE POEMS
IN THIS BOOK

Creativity has always resonated in my mind as a goal to achieve. It makes me feel undoubtfully closer to my creator and deeply connected to the people around me; furthermore, it shows people they're not alone. Humanity experiences your creation and gets to understand a different point of view. People can identify themselves with the author's experience and feel a sense of togetherness and community. There is never a downside to being creative.

The poems in Empathy Prescribed have a common goal: to identify a human experience that might not be as expressed as it should and show the reader that it exists. Once we acknowledge and explain this experience's essence, we can understand each other better and set ways to deal with such issues. But if the abstraction of the matter becomes too overwhelming to a reader, here is an explanation of the poetry in this book.

The Quantification of the World

The Quantification of the World explains how currency came to be. The poem takes us on a journey from the first moment human beings traded their day-by-day hard work into goods and services. It also shows how, because of a way to trade fairly, extremes related to the matter came to be. It creates a distinction between the dark attitude that a greedy person will have versus the self-righteousness of those who tend to think they're not part of a system. These two extremes— greediness and martyrdom— become self-destructive, and end up developing a religion by themselves: a belief that the person's perspective from reality is the only truth.

The Peril of Life

The Peril of Life creates a platform to discuss the constant fight in our minds between religion and humanism. They both have their advantages and disadvantages. Both extremes are unhealthy and impractical.

The first and second stanzas pose the following existentialist question: do we have a purpose in life? The third stanza takes on humanism's flaw: nothing has a purpose, but everything just happens to be. It also exposes religion's judgment and rules. These two elements might end up choking the believer, as opposed to making the person feel saved. Stanza four returns to the topic of humanism and how its lack of purpose sometimes creates an audience of "unbelievers", who feel that no one is in control of their lives. This audience might become stressed and subjective, or dramatic and foolish, as described by the poem. The other show, or point of view, is religion. Religion's extreme might create puppets instead of free-thinkers. Stanza five asks the question to the reader: what do you choose? In the end, the poem concludes that the best way to take on the subject is to be balanced and think of it in terms of a bird of prey. A bird of prey soars high to have a better view, but when needed, it approaches its prey. It suggests impartiality as a means to create balance.

Sober Faith

Sober Faith is a celebration of belief. The poem expresses the need to have healthy, or, as expressed in the poem, sober faith. It criticizes sensationalist faith and instead suggests the type of faith that wouldn't change according to feeling or circumstance.

The first stanza compares the idea of having better faith by not creating false expectations because of desperation. The second stanza refers to the author's important matters about the subject: understanding reality, having a purpose, and focusing on resilience. The third stanza gives an example of what faith looks like; it brings back the moment when the plagues invaded Egypt, according to The Bible. It suggests that, for some people, the plague was certain desperation, but it meant proof of faith to the ones that believed. The following section describes what the author means by "mature faith". It emphasizes the idea that, just like a wound takes its time to heal, so does faith takes time to grow. By demanding a supreme power to execute things at our timing of preference or getting mad at the people around us for our own demise, we show that our faith is not mature. The last stanza ties it all together by advising the reader to choose to have faith that good things will happen, not out of desperation, but regardless of how desperate we are.

Empathy Prescribed

Empathy Prescribed advises the reader on the merits of being empathetic towards others. The poem explains the need and the reason behind empathy and how its opposite feelings can lead to catastrophe.

The first stanza appeals to the reader's identity; if you're empathetic, you will create an environment beneficial to yourself. The opposite is also true; if society doesn't apply empathy, you cannot exist as an individual. The second stanza relates the lack of empathy with war. It describes how war is a consequence and not a cause. War, as described in the poem, is the result of a series of intolerant choices that culminate in the radicalization of society. The fourth stanza describes ignorance also as a consequence and not a cause. It relates ignorance to knowledgeable people's arrogance, who decide to judge those who don't know instead of teaching what they learned. The following section compares the medieval knighthood system (where the apprentice, or squire, was supposed to learn from the knight) to tolerant behavior. It describes the lack of patience from a teacher, whose job is to teach but instead ridicules the student. The last stanza gives a final warning: think before using your words because the world is a fragile place, and peaceful environments need nurturing to exist.

The Sweat on the Brow

The Sweat on the Brow describes the feeling behind hustling. The poem defines the harshness of everyday routine. It explains how desperation can sometimes reach a point where the person who experiences it feels a lack of free choice due to the need. It also describes the workday as full of unpredictability. The poem also shows that complaining doesn't make a difference. Part of our social duty is to pay our debts, a commitment so strong that it's compared to a wedding.

Love Not Deserved

Love Not Deserved describes a love that is not reciprocated, all from the perspective of the person that still loves. The poem takes as inspiration the famous Mexican trio song *Perfidia*.

In the first stanza, the unfortunate lover tells his partner that he has decided to let go of their love. The lover is ready to start the separation process by acknowledging that he doesn't need to know where the person is going. The second stanza describes the partner's attitude towards the lover, how the person's eyes are dead when they see each other. The following paragraph is a cry from the lover's perspective. The lover tells his partner to go and try to wander off to see if they can find what they are looking for. Finally, the poem warns the reader— the lover is afraid that the person's emotional health is at risk, even though he thinks the person is wrong and being vain (at least that is what the lover perceives in the partner every time the partner stays). In the last stanza, the lover finally finds ease through his heartbreak, wishing the best to the person that leaves him behind.

A Sun Dance Ago

When writing this poem, I wanted to describe the creative process. As a fan of creativity myself, I thought of the most straightforward avenue of inspiration through the following question: When do people seem to be enjoying themselves the most? I remember when, as a little girl, I used to have so much fun playing in the garden of my old neighborhood. The garden's configuration was simple but created quite the community feel: there were 27 houses, all surrounding the main park, which was generous in size and vegetation. As a child, the happiest thing was to swirl and dance around such space, without a care in the world. That's how the name of this poem came to be: a sunny day in San José, Costa Rica, full of friends, all twirling around.

The first stanza describes the causes of creativity. Creativity could flow from a dark experience, as well as a joyful moment. Both extremes inspire and impulse the creative mind to act. The following stanza asks the question: How can pain spark the creative process? How can creativity grow amongst pain? The next paragraph lists the ingredients to start the creative process: inspiration, knowledge, courage, and a goal (portraited as the horse who wears blinkers to avoid an involuntary change of direction). The last stanza exalts creativity and compares it to a child's kiss, but not just any child, but a divine offspring, suggesting a heavenly preset on the idea being created.

The Blues

When writing *The Blues* I was inspired by a song by a Hispanic band called Maná. The inspirational song is called "Como Quisiera". The most straight-forward way to translate the title would be "how would I love". The song, considered quite a massive hit in the 90s, starts with a harmonica solo that evokes a nostalgic feeling. I admire any song that will set a mood solely on the base of its sound. The song describes a lover's desire to enjoy solitude by using different metaphors. The poem expresses that same feeling and situation but using a poetic form instead.

The first stanza describes the harmonica sound and how it warms the soul of the person going through heartbreak. The following stanza portrays the guitar's debut in the song, personifying their vibrating movements as the desire to have a lover. The third paragraph depicts the ironic contradiction of a song that might not speak loud to some, but, to the right person, it is loud and echoes certain feelings. This stanza achieves this phenomenon by comparing it to a "loud whisper". The final stanza describes how love songs can make some people feel appreciated and others lonely.

Prejudice

Prejudice came to life while listening to a debate of opposing views. Each person was sure that their idea was 100% correct. At the beginning of the poem, I compare life to a cassette tape. For those of you who are too young to know, a cassette tape is composed mainly of a shiny tape that contains the recordings, fastened by two plastic gears that will fit into the tape recorder to move the tape. The trick is to figure out what to do when the tape got stuck. Regardless of the different ways to fix it; the audio was almost always distorted as a result. Prejudice is portrayed in the same light; once we acquire a stereotypical perspective on a specific matter, it becomes harder to change our mind and open up to new people and ideas.

The first stanza explains this phenomenon by using the cassette tape metaphor. Our perspective surely has flaws, but many times we can't acknowledge those mistakes unless we are open to discussion and prepared to be challenged. The second stanza brings a different metaphor altogether: the process of branding cattle. When branding cattle, the hot iron creates an impression on the cattle's skin that is painful and permanent. It declares ownership of the animal that has it. Prejudice owns the fearful person the same way. It creates a stereotypical idea that is pressed into the person's mind, and as a result, the future has fewer opportunities. The following stanza goes even further by still discussing the fear of the unknown as a mere survival instinct and personifies it into a being that hopes to win his ultimate price: your subjective opinion. The last stanza describes the irony behind a narrow-minded individual, reminding us that if we were all the same people, this world would be unequivocally a boring place.

The Blame

The Blame is the result of politics and COVID. Polarized sides of a given argument have extremes, personas that believe they are unique and complex. In reality, they're the typical selfish person that tries to disguise himself to avoid scrutiny. The first persona discussed is Snobby, who hides in eloquence to avoid telling his constituents that he doesn't have a clue. He applies the dynamic because he enjoys power and respect. The second persona is Neglectful, who is quite the opposite. Neglectful loves to be invisible to avoid responsibility, usually by becoming the victim in need of help. Selfish is the third persona. Selfish is easily identified because he always feels he has the right to live his own life, even if it's detrimental to society. These extreme personas expect and demand respect, becoming nothing else but radical demagogues.

Significance

Significance is the quest of humanity to find value in society. The poem compares this quest to an astronaut's environment by using a series of metaphors related to space.

The first stanza explains that significance cannot be measured. It achieves this by comparing significance to impossible scenarios, like the weight of dust in space (there is no such thing as weight in space) or a shadow in the darkness that ceases to exist (shadows obviously require a degree of light to exist). The second stanza compares the respect and lack of pain (described as void of misuse) of a person who has achieved significance in their life to research about a far-away celestial body. The cosmic body value is such that it's worth spending endless resources on. The following verses ask the questions: how do we find significance? How do we survive the toll it takes to achieve such nirvana state? The poem supplies a simple answer: we become brave enough to try something, even if it means a sure fail and a costly fall. The last passage describes how rare it is for some people to have a sense of being important to society and how common it is to others. The fragment explains how the astronaut considers his ordeal of ordinary relevance, but to the viewer, the idea of becoming an astronaut could be impossible to imagine.

Kaleidoscopic Joy

In my own quest to achieve happiness in life, I find myself asking a simple question: If a person were to ask me how to be happy, how would I respond? Well, the best way to explain an abstract feeling, in my opinion, is through the use of imagery. When one compares Joy to a simple toy, like a Kaleidoscope, it helps create a base to convey a point. The lesson of the poem is simple: Joy is more a choice than a circumstance.

The first stanza describes a Kaleidoscope and its final purpose: to create whimsical figures and wake up joy inside ourselves. The second stanza compares Joy's attributes to a scene at a carnival, where a child happens to meet an old-time friend. They easily and freely enjoy life by just playing together. The following passage digs deeper into the utopian state of permanent happiness, where there is no want, and everything is as it should be. Furthermore, the third stanza asks the reader how to achieve joy while comparing its quest to a toymaker who creates a kaleidoscope. The final section gives the ultimate lesson: it's mostly about the decision to be happy, just like a kaleidoscope, which in reality is just an optical illusion that wouldn't be interesting if it wasn't for our mood to have fun with it.

Elegy

Elegy is the story of a family who just lost their patriarch to disease. I have personally experienced this in my life. As I wrote this poem, I often asked my younger brother's input, who was the most devastated by my father's death, since he was just a teenager at the time it happened.

The first stanza sets the tone— the family was having dinner when they received the terrible news of their father's declining health. The second portion further explains the feeling behind the abandoned supper on the table. It describes how it wasn't a family argument due to unimportant matters. It was merely the fact that no one could continue eating because the news was so hard to take. The third stanza reveals the terrible news to the reader: there is a death in the family. Paragraph four describes the anxiety behind the dreadful event— the beating of the chest, the uncertainty, and the anguish of knowing that the father died. According to the poem, the death of a father is not only about missing a loved one; it's also about knowing that the person you relied on the most in life is not there to help you navigate through it anymore. Still, the family wishes that maybe something is mistaken, and the father isn't dead. Stanza five describes what happens the day after a death. It defines the burial ritual: the black dresses, the decisions, and the commotion of a burial. The last stanza shows the experience in a positive light: the privilege the family had in having an exemplary father in a world full of men who don't want to be one.

Jazz Under the Rain

Jazz Under the Rain is based on the life experiences of my daughter as a college student. She was walking towards the campus library one day when, all of a sudden, it started to rain. She remembers getting her sneakers all wet, and at that moment, she decided not to let her currently wet outfit ruin the day. So, as easy going as she usually is, she put her air pods on and listened to her favorite music genre, which is Jazz (Chet Baker seems to always do the trick for her).

The first stanza describes her pace and personality. She walks with a certain speed that can only be described as "cadence pace", for her petite figure doesn't allow her to extend her legs beyond a certain point. She looks like a typical college student, but inside she has a big heart and willingness to help the people in need. The second stanza describes the scene a little further, explaining how she was carrying her umbrella in a narrow path on her college campus and how her mind is fixed on her two most challenging subjects at the moment: biology and math. Section three is self-explanatory; it's a description of how she looked and her attitude towards life at that moment. The following paragraph is about her mentality behind the scene—a person with a goal in her mind. This goal might take her to the limit, and still, she sings in the rain... indeed a memorable moment. The last stanza describes the environment with a little more detail and reassures the reader that she intends to achieve her heart's desires.

Grit

I have always considered the medical profession highly altruistic. It is very sacrificial; but medic soldiers, emergency transit staff, firefighters... they are the most sacrificial people one can think of. *Grit* is a tribute to that type of sacrifice.

The first stanza describes how, even when the battle seems lost, the first responder will still insist on saving a life until there is nothing left to save. Stanza two describes how a soldier, including the medical units, would feel in a battle that might be lost. They feel impotence because they can't save everyone. They feel hurt because they see friends and unit members that are in pain. Still, they manage to keep it together and go on saving lives. The third stanza describes how demoralizing war is but how enriching the brotherhood between soldiers can be. It also explains the mental battle of a first responder soldier and how they change their mentality to avoid thinking catastrophically for the mission's sake. The last stanza gives a valuable lesson on a first responder soldier's attitude: they know their limitations, but never how to quit.

Summer's off

This poem describes the evolution from summer to fall compared to a child's transition to become a grown-up.

The first stanza explains the weather pattern of the arrival of fall and creates a metaphor about a child's mind that starts to change to face the reality of existentialism. The second stanza describes how the child slowly stops his playful manners to become aware and understand his own mind and the world around him. The third stanza states that when responsibility becomes a part of the child's life, he has to become a different person. The final stanza places a metaphor to link how the days become shorter as winter approaches with the child's coming of age.

Juniper Sea

Juniper Sea is the sad story of a superficial woman who had it all during her youth, and how she later became a grumpy and isolated person. Even though this story might be every adult's worst fear, it is portrayed to create awareness of the dangers of superficial relationships.

The poem starts by describing Juniper's luxurious life in her youth: her lavish parties, her fancy attitude, and how her priorities weren't in the right order. In the second section, we see how Juniper always hired live music for her parties, but now she sits alone to drink her tea. The third paragraph explains the moment her friends forgot Juniper. Juniper got sick with a disease that ended up being too costly and damaging to her previously glamorous face. After suffering from this terrible illness, Juniper realized her mostly superficial friends abandoned her because she was now tight on money and not a pretty sight herself. Finally, Juniper's greatest fear materializes: society now sees her as an imperfect human being, forcing her to isolate herself out of pride and pain. This whole ordeal made her senile to the point where she simply didn't want to live in the present, for it was too painful. Her mind wandered off to the past without ever returning.

Once in a Blue Moon

Once in a Blue Moon is a poem on how to take advantage of every opportunity life has to offer.

The poem starts by explaining how ideas are created, regardless of the time of day. Secondly, the poem gives the reader sound advice: shut your eyes to fear of rejection or pain. The lesson is also to work hard, for the idea alone cannot accomplish anything. The process of expressing the idea begins, and so the fear of failure. I decided to explain these feelings by using a metaphor of a train going full speed. The train suddenly needs to switch lanes to survive a crash. Stopping the train seems like the easiest way to avoid a disaster. But if we stopped our train, how would we figure out if it was ever worth the risk? The last stanza gives final advice: opportunity is rare, so, take the risk, even though the odds might seem against you. Even if you fail to achieve what you set yourself to do, you will have earned self-respect and resilience.

The Synthesis of You and Me

The Synthesis of You and Me describes the beauty of a perfect relationship of two people in love. In the first stanza, I compared a good relationship with my trip through Italy during the summer of 2017. Part of the trip was a visit to a little medieval village over the Tuscan hills called Volterra, known in the ancient world to be a massive alabaster quarry. Volterra has an elevated altitude, which was quite advantageous during attacks or raids back in the day. Nowadays, this magnificent view is merely a tourist attraction, but this sight over the Tuscan hills is incomparable. The poem's first stanza describes a sunset scene in Volterra: great food with my favorite people in the world, an excellent view, and perfect weather. Relaxation and enjoyment involving all senses, that's how the poem describes a healthy relationship. The following stanza compares a good relationship with our time in Rome. Rome is captivating. Everywhere you look, there is an exciting structure that catches your eye, especially ancient ruins. We spend several days there, where we had no setbacks or work to do. Budget is a big part of Europe's enjoyment since it lets you have better choices on hotels, restaurants, and tour options, so the poem pinpoints the ideal situation of not having to worry about expenses. The third stanza also explains how the perfect trip wouldn't be complete without the health and energy to walk the long distances, comparing all of this to an idyllic bond between a couple. In the end, the last stanza conveys a powerful point: a healthy relationship is not just about good experiences but compares perfect love to a chemical bond, where two chemicals become one, impossible to separate. Love, in the end, is our human intent to eradicate sorrow out of life.

The Zombie of Me

While watching the movie *Venom*, I thought to myself: what feeling in life will captivate a human being in such a way as to knowingly become self-destructive? After creating a list of several attitudes that result in this terrible fruit, I realized that most of these characteristics were invisible to the human eye. There are seldom attitudes, however, that anyone can detect in a person by just looking at their behavior for a bit, and the worst of them, in my opinion, is vanity. Vanity is rooted in the evil concept of narcissism. It requires the person to be egotistical by definition— a deserver of all eyes and ears. A vain person fishes for complements for the sole purpose of making the point that he or she is better than you. So, while the arrogant person believes him or herself to be on the top of the mountain, in reality, the people around them are finding the whole charade very distasteful.

The first stanza describes how vanity takes ownership of its host— like a parasite that feeds from its host's conscience or better judgment. The second section gives a name to such parasite: vanity. It describes it as enchanting at first but eventually making its host a slave. The third stanza describes how vanity comes to be. The creature of vanity compares for the sake of winning a competition, regardless of how relevant the matter in the discussion is or how devastating the conversation could become to the other person involved. The following paragraph describes a vain individual's social perception: a person who believes they smell delicious, but in reality, everyone gossips on how ridiculously stinky this person is. It describes a vain person as a self-absorbed individual who doesn't notice his or her flaws. The last stanza gives a stark warning to the reader: even though vanity seems obvious and damaging to its witnesses, it can still create a follower of anyone, myself included, at any given moment in time.

Blue

Blue is the cry of the oceans and rivers to be saved from pollution. Few things resonate with every human being on earth as much as the importance of the water condition. In this poem, I strove to give human emotion to the water in the oceans and rivers. I do so by attributing its beauty and behavior to an intentional need to communicate: an appeal to humanity to control pollution. During my whole life, I have been exposed to coastal living— first as a Costa Rican, visiting the beaches during my childhood, and now as a Florida resident, practically living most of my life no further than two hours away from the sea. For this reason, I emphasize the importance of keeping water clean.

The first stanza starts by asking the reader some fundamental questions: Is the water's color still blue, as it should be? Is water, as a personified object, trying to tell us that it is getting sick? Is the behavior of water a consequence of our inaction to care for it? Is the color of the water changing because of pollution? In the end, the poem agrees with the water as if it has a convincing argument: humanity has to change its behavior. The poem gives damning evidence of this point of view by showing pollution on the shores; hence, water is right; it has been mistreated.

Desert's Displeasure

Desert's Displeasure is the avid description of life's mental struggles through the metaphor of the different types of desert bodies on earth. In this poem, I used the word desert as equivalent to trials in life.

The first stanza expresses the feelings behind a life's trial: a situation that seems hopeless and aleatory, but most of all, a mandatory experience if one is to live life at its fullest. The first desert explained is the coastal desert, exemplified by the Atacama Desert in South America. The idea that a body of water is so close to a desert is very ironic. If, for example, a person got lost in a coastal desert, that person will always know the direction to set eyes on by spotting the sea. Life has similar situations— circumstances where you have a goal that is out of reach. That is the definition of frustration, where an occasion in life is not what one expected, and patience has run out when finding a solution. No matter how much we try to find an answer, it appears to not be within our grasp.

The second stanza is about The Sahara Desert. There is no sense of direction in this arid desert but miles and miles of sand and heat. Life has moments when we find ourselves lost. What could have started as a plan with a clear goal could potentially become a failure, as we lose sight of our actions' purpose. Consequently, we develop stress and anxiety, a fear of not knowing where we're heading and what is to come.

The last desert explained in the poem is the cold desert of Antarctica. This stanza relates such cold weather with loneliness. It expresses how sometimes we become invisible to society, not feeling cared for or loved by anyone around us. In return, this feeling of neglect leaves us with no one to care for, making ourselves question our purpose in life. It makes us feel numb like the numbness felt during frostbite. The last stanza explains the importance of resilience. The lesson being that pain equips us to be more loving, understanding, and helpful towards others.

Steadfast Wind

Steadfast Wind plays with the idea of the negative effect of comfort in society. I often tell my son that life can bring success or a lesson, but never a failure. When life becomes too comfortable, we might stagnate growth because we aren't experiencing defeat. The first stanza plays with this concept, arguing that comfort's consequence is to not grow emotionally as human beings. We sacrifice our better version of ourselves when things go right. We don't learn, for we aren't required to do so.

The second stanza explains why: a person with nothing to lose is not going to make an effort to improve. We might try to, but there is no need. The following verses refer to what happens when confronted with a storm in our lives; we prepare ourselves to avoid a terrible outcome. The fourth stanza establishes the metaphor by explaining to the reader that comfort makes a drug out of safety and harmony. Comfort is addictive; the more we find ourselves in comfort, the more we crave for it, and the more we fear change. The last stanza is a lesson in prejudice: we can all agree on such a point of view, but we can also agree that we will try to dodge the bullet of an uncomfortable situation. Finally, the reader is left with the idea that life would become pointless if our sole purpose is to avoid pain.

Old libel

Old libel is a poem about an old argument between love ones. The poem reflects on the idea that even though the sound of words is not permanent, the impact of what is said could spark again at any moment's notice and recreate the feeling. The poem first explains this previous phenomenon by comparing it to the wind. The wind takes the sound of words without asking the person who's emitting the sound— the wind steals the words away.

The second section describes the terrible words said by one of the people involved in the conversation. The contrast between an old, tasteless meal and the words the person said helps the reader understand this devastating effect. The following stanza describes one of the narrator's selfish points in the conversation and how his paranoia has led them to question the motives behind the other person's words. What were love and harmony now become a twisted relationship because of an old argument that resurfaced.

Thief at Night

Thief at Night is a poem about the mentality of a thief while stealing.

The first stanza describes the thief's attitude. The thief is restless and quiet, about to start his terrible act. Next, the poem points at envy as the reason behind a theft. The insistent justification of a thief is the belief that he deserves someone else's possessions. Ultimately, this justification meets greed and turns a person into a beast. The third stanza describes the behavior of the beast, an animal devouring his prey. While the incident is happening, the victim pretends to be sleeping in bed for the sole purpose of life preservation. Lastly the poem describes to the reader the aftermath of a robbery: possessions are gone, and instead, a heart full of fear and trauma, which will take time to heal.

ACKNOWLEDGMENTS

No goal is achievable without teamwork. Every knowledgeable academic, every prosperous business person, and every successful philanthropist all have a common element in their lives: a team of supporters who held them in times of need and cheered them in times of success. As for myself, even though my simple goal was to publish *Empathy Prescribed*, I do have many people to thank. First and foremost, my family who helped me when I was too busy to even take care of myself. To my son Samuel, who consistently read my every poem and took my work seriously since the beginning. To my husband Roy, for his willingness to change the household dynamic for the sake of this book (and my happiness). To my daughter and personal cheerleader Priscilla, for encouraging me to write and read.

I deeply indebted to my mother, for having the vision to register me in one of the most challenging bilingual schools in Costa Rica, in a time when the society around her and her personal struggles could have easily convinced her otherwise.

Thanks to my friend Julie Vargas from The Creative Jungle Photography Studio for believing in my writing. I greatly appreciate you taking that emblematic shot that later became the author's picture. A special thanks to Sergio Garzón for his imaginative illustrations, to Richard L. Joenes for his amazing creativity while making the cover of the book, to Jenny Xu for her honest editorial skills, and to Archway Publishing for their patience in guiding me through this unique adventure of publishing a poetry book.

Lastly, I wish to thank my brother Fernando and his business Tux Solutions, for creating a brand and web content worthy of a billion-dollar firm; extra patience and time included.

Finally, a shout out to my conscious self for learning how to pull up with my unconscious self... good work you two!

Lightning Source UK Ltd.
Milton Keynes UK
UKHW041850250221
379413UK00008B/517/J